Podcast Name

PODCAST PLANNER
[Worksheets for 50 Shows]
& QUICKSTART GUIDE

Fun & Freebies!
BadPermUnicorn.com
Funny Adult
Coloring Books & More!

For more information, contact author or publishing company:
info@BadPermUnicorn.com | www.BadPermUnicorn.com

Blah, blah, blah. MOST important....**Thank You for supporting our wacky side hustle!** Transforming nutty ideas into fun books is a blast. Happy podcasting!

‖‖‖ Contents ‖‖‖

EPISODE TITLE		EPISODE #	DURATION	PUBLISH DATE

🎤 QuickStart Guide

TOPIC/THEME	GUEST(s)	CONTACT INFO

🎙️ SHOW INTRO

- Quickly convey show's unique value proposition.
- Why is show the best option for your unique listeners? Snappy taglines are awesome.
- Brief, bold show summaries are key.
- Briefly introduce yourself. Powerful 1-2 sentence bio reinforces why you are the only one to host show.

☆ GUEST/TOPIC INTRO

- Hook & hold listeners with brief, engaging summary.
- Create open loop. Ask a question which will be answered within the show.
- For guests/interviews, include a short, wow-worthy introduction.
- Dazzle with accomplishments. Why should they listen?

💬 QUESTIONS

- Avoid Yes/No Questions
- Put a Face to Facts. Personalize Dry Stats.
- Ask "Why" & "How" to Reveal Feelings
- Research your Way to Good Questions
- Know Where Interview is Going & Prepare for Detours
- Actively Listen! Follow-Up Questions are Key to Good Interviews
- [Read "Interview Tips" Chapter]

- Extra Guest or Topic Info
- Sources of Guest/Topic Info
- Timecode of Good Soundbites
- Bumper Music Ideas/Sources
- Important Show Notes
- Other Info/Links Mentioned
- Promote Guest's Website/Socials

SPONSOR INFO

PODCAST ((♀)) WORKFLOW

GUEST

IDENTIFY & BOOK ○

SEND PODCAST INFO ○

SET RECORDING DATE ○

DATE _____ TIME _____

RECORD EPISODE _____ ○

EDIT EPISODE _____ ○

**SHOW NOTES/
ARTWORK** _____ ○

PUBLISH EPISODE _____ ○

PROMOTE EPISODE _____ ○

EPISODE TITLE		EPISODE #	DURATION	PUBLISH DATE

TOPIC/THEME	GUEST(s)	CONTACT INFO

🎙 SHOW INTRO

_____
_____
_____
_____
_____
_____

☆ GUEST/TOPIC INTRO

_____
_____
_____
_____
_____
_____

💬 QUESTIONS

_____
_____
_____
_____
_____
_____
_____
_____
_____
_____
_____

✎ NOTES

_____

_____

_____

_____

_____

_____

_____

_____

_____

_____

_____

_____

_____

_____

_____

_____

_____

_____

_____

_____

✕ SPONSOR INFO

PODCAST ((ᴘ)) WORKFLOW

GUEST

    IDENTIFY & BOOK ◯

    SEND PODCAST INFO ◯

    SET RECORDING DATE ◯

    DATE _____ TIME _____

RECORD EPISODE _____ ◯

EDIT EPISODE _____ ◯

SHOW NOTES/ ARTWORK _____ ◯

PUBLISH EPISODE _____ ◯

PROMOTE EPISODE _____ ◯

_____ _____

_____ _____

EPISODE TITLE		EPISODE #	DURATION	PUBLISH DATE

TOPIC/THEME	GUEST(s)	CONTACT INFO

🎙 SHOW INTRO

⭐ GUEST/TOPIC INTRO

💬 QUESTIONS

_____

_____

_____

_____

_____

_____

_____

_____

_____

_____

_____

_____

_____

_____

_____

_____

_____

_____

_____

⋇ SPONSOR INFO

PODCAST ((ᵩ)) WORKFLOW

GUEST

    IDENTIFY & BOOK   ◯

    SEND PODCAST INFO   ◯

    SET RECORDING DATE   ◯

    DATE _____ TIME _____

RECORD EPISODE _____ ◯

EDIT EPISODE _____ ◯

**SHOW NOTES/
ARTWORK** _____ ◯

PUBLISH EPISODE _____ ◯

PROMOTE EPISODE _____ ◯

_____

_____

EPISODE TITLE		EPISODE #	DURATION	PUBLISH DATE

TOPIC/THEME	GUEST(s)	CONTACT INFO

🎙 SHOW INTRO

_____

_____

_____

_____

_____

_____

☆ GUEST/TOPIC INTRO

_____

_____

_____

_____

_____

_____

💬 QUESTIONS

_____

_____

_____

_____

_____

_____

_____

_____

_____

_____

_____

_____

SPONSOR INFO

PODCAST ((ọ)) WORKFLOW

GUEST

IDENTIFY & BOOK ◯

SEND PODCAST INFO ◯

SET RECORDING DATE ◯

DATE _____ TIME _____

RECORD EPISODE _____ ◯

EDIT EPISODE _____ ◯

SHOW NOTES/ ARTWORK _____ ◯

PUBLISH EPISODE _____ ◯

PROMOTE EPISODE _____ ◯

EPISODE TITLE		EPISODE #	DURATION	PUBLISH DATE

TOPIC/THEME	GUEST(s)	CONTACT INFO

🎙 SHOW INTRO

_____
_____
_____
_____
_____
_____

☆ GUEST/TOPIC INTRO

_____
_____
_____
_____
_____

💬 QUESTIONS

_____
_____
_____
_____
_____
_____
_____
_____
_____
_____
_____

✎ NOTES

_____
_____
_____
_____
_____
_____
_____
_____
_____
_____
_____
_____
_____
_____
_____
_____
_____
_____
_____

⌁ SPONSOR INFO

PODCAST ((ϙ)) WORKFLOW

GUEST

IDENTIFY & BOOK ⭕

SEND PODCAST INFO ⭕

SET RECORDING DATE ⭕

DATE _____ TIME _____

RECORD EPISODE _____ ⭕

EDIT EPISODE _____ ⭕

**SHOW NOTES/
ARTWORK** _____ ⭕

PUBLISH EPISODE _____ ⭕

PROMOTE EPISODE _____ ⭕

_____
_____

EPISODE TITLE		EPISODE #	DURATION	PUBLISH DATE

TOPIC/THEME	GUEST(s)	CONTACT INFO

🎙 SHOW INTRO

_____
_____
_____
_____
_____
_____

⭐ GUEST/TOPIC INTRO

_____
_____
_____
_____
_____
_____

💬 QUESTIONS

_____
_____
_____
_____
_____
_____
_____
_____
_____
_____
_____
_____

✎ NOTES

_____

_____

_____

_____

_____

_____

_____

_____

_____

_____

_____

_____

_____

_____

_____

_____

_____

_____

_____

_____

_____

✧ SPONSOR INFO

PODCAST ((ꞯ)) WORKFLOW

GUEST

    IDENTIFY & BOOK ⃝

    SEND PODCAST INFO ⃝

    SET RECORDING DATE ⃝

    DATE _____ TIME _____

RECORD EPISODE _____ ⃝

EDIT EPISODE _____ ⃝

SHOW NOTES/ ARTWORK _____ ⃝

PUBLISH EPISODE _____ ⃝

PROMOTE EPISODE _____ ⃝

_____

_____

EPISODE TITLE		EPISODE #	DURATION	PUBLISH DATE

TOPIC/THEME	GUEST(s)	CONTACT INFO

🎙 SHOW INTRO

⭐ GUEST/TOPIC INTRO

💬 QUESTIONS

✏️ NOTES

_____

_____

_____

_____

_____

_____

_____

_____

_____

_____

_____

_____

_____

_____

_____

_____

_____

_____

⌁ SPONSOR INFO

PODCAST ((ၐ)) WORKFLOW

GUEST

IDENTIFY & BOOK ◯

SEND PODCAST INFO ◯

SET RECORDING DATE ◯

DATE _____ TIME _____

RECORD EPISODE _____ ◯

EDIT EPISODE _____ ◯

SHOW NOTES/ ARTWORK _____ ◯

PUBLISH EPISODE _____ ◯

PROMOTE EPISODE _____ ◯

_____

_____

EPISODE TITLE		EPISODE #	DURATION	PUBLISH DATE

TOPIC/THEME	GUEST(s)	CONTACT INFO

🎙 SHOW INTRO

_____
_____
_____
_____
_____
_____

☆ GUEST/TOPIC INTRO

_____
_____
_____
_____
_____
_____

💬 QUESTIONS

_____
_____
_____
_____
_____
_____
_____
_____
_____
_____
_____
_____

NOTES

_____

_____

_____

_____

_____

_____

_____

_____

_____

_____

_____

_____

_____

_____

_____

_____

_____

_____

_____

_____

SPONSOR INFO

PODCAST WORKFLOW

GUEST

    IDENTIFY & BOOK ⭘

    SEND PODCAST INFO ⭘

    SET RECORDING DATE ⭘

    DATE _____ TIME _____

RECORD EPISODE _____ ⭘

EDIT EPISODE _____ ⭘

SHOW NOTES/ ARTWORK _____ ⭘

PUBLISH EPISODE _____ ⭘

PROMOTE EPISODE _____ ⭘

_____

_____

EPISODE TITLE		EPISODE #	DURATION	PUBLISH DATE

TOPIC/THEME	GUEST(s)	CONTACT INFO

🎙 SHOW INTRO

_____
_____
_____
_____
_____
_____
_____

☆ GUEST/TOPIC INTRO

_____
_____
_____
_____
_____
_____
_____

💬 QUESTIONS

_____
_____
_____
_____
_____
_____
_____
_____
_____
_____
_____
_____
_____

NOTES

_____
_____
_____
_____
_____
_____
_____
_____
_____
_____
_____
_____
_____
_____
_____
_____
_____
_____
_____
_____
_____
_____

SPONSOR INFO

PODCAST ((ɸ)) WORKFLOW

GUEST

IDENTIFY & BOOK ◯

SEND PODCAST INFO ◯

SET RECORDING DATE ◯

DATE _____ TIME _____

RECORD EPISODE _____ ◯

EDIT EPISODE _____ ◯

**SHOW NOTES/
ARTWORK** _____ ◯

PUBLISH EPISODE _____ ◯

PROMOTE EPISODE _____ ◯

_____
_____

EPISODE TITLE		EPISODE #	DURATION	PUBLISH DATE

TOPIC/THEME	GUEST(s)	CONTACT INFO

🎙 SHOW INTRO

☆ GUEST/TOPIC INTRO

💬 QUESTIONS

✎ NOTES

_____

_____

_____

_____

_____

_____

_____

_____

_____

_____

_____

_____

_____

_____

_____

_____

_____

_____

_____

⤜ SPONSOR INFO

PODCAST ((ᵖ)) WORKFLOW

GUEST

    IDENTIFY & BOOK ⬭

    SEND PODCAST INFO ⬭

    SET RECORDING DATE ⬭

    DATE _____ TIME _____

RECORD EPISODE _____ ⬭

EDIT EPISODE _____ ⬭

**SHOW NOTES/
ARTWORK** _____ ⬭

PUBLISH EPISODE _____ ⬭

PROMOTE EPISODE _____ ⬭

_____

_____

EPISODE TITLE		EPISODE #	DURATION	PUBLISH DATE

TOPIC/THEME	GUEST(s)	CONTACT INFO

🎤 SHOW INTRO

☆ GUEST/TOPIC INTRO

💬 QUESTIONS

✏️ **NOTES**

_____
_____
_____
_____
_____
_____
_____
_____
_____
_____
_____
_____
_____
_____
_____
_____
_____
_____
_____
_____

SPONSOR INFO

PODCAST ((ϙ)) WORKFLOW

GUEST

    IDENTIFY & BOOK ◯

    SEND PODCAST INFO ◯

    SET RECORDING DATE ◯

    DATE _____ TIME _____

RECORD EPISODE _____ ◯

EDIT EPISODE _____ ◯

SHOW NOTES/ ARTWORK _____ ◯

PUBLISH EPISODE _____ ◯

PROMOTE EPISODE _____ ◯

_____
_____

EPISODE TITLE		EPISODE #	DURATION	PUBLISH DATE

TOPIC/THEME	GUEST(s)	CONTACT INFO

🎤 SHOW INTRO

_____
_____
_____
_____
_____
_____

⭐ GUEST/TOPIC INTRO

_____
_____
_____
_____
_____
_____

💬 QUESTIONS

_____
_____
_____
_____
_____
_____
_____
_____
_____
_____
_____
_____
_____

_____

_____

_____

_____

_____

_____

_____

_____

_____

_____

_____

_____

_____

_____

_____

_____

_____

_____

_____

_____

⦵ SPONSOR INFO

PODCAST ((ꝑ)) WORKFLOW

GUEST

IDENTIFY & BOOK ◯

SEND PODCAST INFO ◯

SET RECORDING DATE ◯

DATE _____ TIME _____

RECORD EPISODE _____ ◯

EDIT EPISODE _____ ◯

SHOW NOTES/ ARTWORK _____ ◯

PUBLISH EPISODE _____ ◯

PROMOTE EPISODE _____ ◯

_____

_____

EPISODE TITLE		EPISODE #	DURATION	PUBLISH DATE

TOPIC/THEME	GUEST(s)		CONTACT INFO

🎙 SHOW INTRO

⭐ GUEST/TOPIC INTRO

💬 QUESTIONS

⌁ **SPONSOR INFO**

PODCAST ((ᵩ)) WORKFLOW

GUEST

    IDENTIFY & BOOK ◯

    SEND PODCAST INFO ◯

    SET RECORDING DATE ◯

    DATE _____ TIME _____

RECORD EPISODE _____ ◯

EDIT EPISODE _____ ◯

SHOW NOTES/ ARTWORK _____ ◯

PUBLISH EPISODE _____ ◯

PROMOTE EPISODE _____ ◯

EPISODE TITLE		EPISODE #	DURATION	PUBLISH DATE

TOPIC/THEME	GUEST(s)	CONTACT INFO

🎙 SHOW INTRO

☆ GUEST/TOPIC INTRO

💬 QUESTIONS

✐ NOTES

_____
_____
_____
_____
_____
_____
_____
_____
_____
_____
_____
_____
_____
_____
_____
_____
_____
_____
_____

✕ SPONSOR INFO

PODCAST ((ɸ)) WORKFLOW

GUEST

    IDENTIFY & BOOK ⃝

    SEND PODCAST INFO ⃝

    SET RECORDING DATE ⃝

    DATE _____ TIME _____

RECORD EPISODE _____ ⃝

EDIT EPISODE _____ ⃝

SHOW NOTES/ ARTWORK _____ ⃝

PUBLISH EPISODE _____ ⃝

PROMOTE EPISODE _____ ⃝

_____ _____

_____ _____

EPISODE TITLE		EPISODE #	DURATION	PUBLISH DATE

TOPIC/THEME	GUEST(s)	CONTACT INFO

🎙 SHOW INTRO

_____
_____
_____
_____
_____
_____

☆ GUEST/TOPIC INTRO

_____
_____
_____
_____
_____
_____

💬 QUESTIONS

_____
_____
_____
_____
_____
_____
_____
_____
_____
_____
_____
_____

✎ NOTES

✕ SPONSOR INFO

PODCAST ((ʔ)) WORKFLOW

GUEST

IDENTIFY & BOOK ⭘

SEND PODCAST INFO ⭘

SET RECORDING DATE ⭘

DATE _____ TIME _____

RECORD EPISODE _____ ⭘

EDIT EPISODE _____ ⭘

**SHOW NOTES/
ARTWORK** _____ ⭘

PUBLISH EPISODE _____ ⭘

PROMOTE EPISODE _____ ⭘

EPISODE TITLE		EPISODE #	DURATION	PUBLISH DATE

TOPIC/THEME	GUEST(s)	CONTACT INFO

🎙 SHOW INTRO

⭐ GUEST/TOPIC INTRO

💬 QUESTIONS

PODCAST ((ͦ)) WORKFLOW

GUEST

IDENTIFY & BOOK ◯

SEND PODCAST INFO ◯

SET RECORDING DATE ◯

DATE _____ TIME _____

RECORD EPISODE _____ ◯

EDIT EPISODE _____ ◯

**SHOW NOTES/
ARTWORK** _____ ◯

PUBLISH EPISODE _____ ◯

PROMOTE EPISODE _____ ◯

_____

_____

EPISODE TITLE		EPISODE #	DURATION	PUBLISH DATE

TOPIC/THEME	GUEST(s)	CONTACT INFO

🎙 SHOW INTRO

_____
_____
_____
_____
_____
_____

☆ GUEST/TOPIC INTRO

_____
_____
_____
_____
_____

💬 QUESTIONS

_____
_____
_____
_____
_____
_____
_____
_____
_____
_____
_____

✎ NOTES

(blank lined note space)

⤙ SPONSOR INFO

PODCAST ((ᵠ)) WORKFLOW

GUEST

    IDENTIFY & BOOK ○

    SEND PODCAST INFO ○

    SET RECORDING DATE ○

    DATE _____ TIME _____

RECORD EPISODE _____ ○

EDIT EPISODE _____ ○

SHOW NOTES/ARTWORK _____ ○

PUBLISH EPISODE _____ ○

PROMOTE EPISODE _____ ○

_____

_____

EPISODE TITLE		EPISODE #	DURATION	PUBLISH DATE

TOPIC/THEME	GUEST(s)	CONTACT INFO

🎙 SHOW INTRO

_____

_____

_____

_____

_____

☆ GUEST/TOPIC INTRO

_____

_____

_____

_____

_____

💬 QUESTIONS

_____

_____

_____

_____

_____

_____

_____

_____

_____

_____

✎ NOTES

⌀ SPONSOR INFO

PODCAST ((ᵱ)) WORKFLOW

GUEST

IDENTIFY & BOOK ◯

SEND PODCAST INFO ◯

SET RECORDING DATE ◯

DATE _____ TIME _____

RECORD EPISODE _____ ◯

EDIT EPISODE _____ ◯

SHOW NOTES/ ARTWORK _____ ◯

PUBLISH EPISODE _____ ◯

PROMOTE EPISODE _____ ◯

EPISODE TITLE		EPISODE #	DURATION	PUBLISH DATE

TOPIC/THEME	GUEST(s)		CONTACT INFO

🎙 SHOW INTRO

_____
_____
_____
_____
_____
_____

☆ GUEST/TOPIC INTRO

_____
_____
_____
_____
_____
_____

💬 QUESTIONS

_____
_____
_____
_____
_____
_____
_____
_____
_____
_____
_____
_____

NOTES

_____

_____

_____

_____

_____

_____

_____

_____

_____

_____

_____

_____

_____

_____

_____

_____

_____

_____

_____

_____

SPONSOR INFO

PODCAST ((ϙ)) WORKFLOW

GUEST

IDENTIFY & BOOK ◯

SEND PODCAST INFO ◯

SET RECORDING DATE ◯

DATE _____ TIME _____

RECORD EPISODE _____ ◯

EDIT EPISODE _____ ◯

SHOW NOTES/ ARTWORK _____ ◯

PUBLISH EPISODE _____ ◯

PROMOTE EPISODE _____ ◯

_____

_____

EPISODE TITLE		EPISODE #	DURATION	PUBLISH DATE

TOPIC/THEME	GUEST(s)	CONTACT INFO

🎙 SHOW INTRO

_____
_____
_____
_____
_____
_____

☆ GUEST/TOPIC INTRO

_____
_____
_____
_____
_____

💬 QUESTIONS

_____
_____
_____
_____
_____
_____
_____
_____
_____
_____
_____

✎ NOTES

_____

_____

_____

_____

_____

_____

_____

_____

_____

_____

_____

_____

_____

_____

_____

_____

_____

_____

_____

_____

_____

⤜ SPONSOR INFO	PODCAST ((ᵖ)) WORKFLOW
	GUEST
	IDENTIFY & BOOK ◯
	SEND PODCAST INFO ◯
	SET RECORDING DATE ◯
	DATE _____ TIME _____
	RECORD EPISODE _____ ◯
	EDIT EPISODE _____ ◯
	SHOW NOTES/ ARTWORK _____ ◯
	PUBLISH EPISODE _____ ◯
	PROMOTE EPISODE _____ ◯
	_____
	_____

EPISODE TITLE		EPISODE #	DURATION	PUBLISH DATE

TOPIC/THEME	GUEST(s)	CONTACT INFO

🎙 SHOW INTRO

_____

_____

_____

_____

_____

_____

⭐ GUEST/TOPIC INTRO

_____

_____

_____

_____

_____

_____

💬 QUESTIONS

_____

_____

_____

_____

_____

_____

_____

_____

_____

_____

_____

_____

SPONSOR INFO

PODCAST ((♀)) WORKFLOW

GUEST

IDENTIFY & BOOK ○

SEND PODCAST INFO ○

SET RECORDING DATE ○

DATE _____ TIME _____

RECORD EPISODE _____ ○

EDIT EPISODE _____ ○

**SHOW NOTES/
ARTWORK** _____ ○

PUBLISH EPISODE _____ ○

PROMOTE EPISODE _____ ○

EPISODE TITLE		EPISODE #	DURATION	PUBLISH DATE

TOPIC/THEME	GUEST(s)	CONTACT INFO

🎙 **SHOW INTRO**

_____
_____
_____
_____
_____
_____
_____

⭐ **GUEST/TOPIC INTRO**

_____
_____
_____
_____
_____
_____

💬 **QUESTIONS**

_____
_____
_____
_____
_____
_____
_____
_____
_____
_____
_____
_____

NOTES

_____
_____
_____
_____
_____
_____
_____
_____
_____
_____
_____
_____
_____
_____
_____
_____
_____
_____
_____
_____

SPONSOR INFO

PODCAST ((φ)) WORKFLOW

GUEST

IDENTIFY & BOOK ○

SEND PODCAST INFO ○

SET RECORDING DATE ○

DATE _____ TIME _____

RECORD EPISODE _____ ○

EDIT EPISODE _____ ○

**SHOW NOTES/
ARTWORK** _____ ○

PUBLISH EPISODE _____ ○

PROMOTE EPISODE _____ ○

_____
_____

EPISODE TITLE		EPISODE #	DURATION	PUBLISH DATE

TOPIC/THEME	GUEST(s)	CONTACT INFO

🎙 SHOW INTRO

⭐ GUEST/TOPIC INTRO

💬 QUESTIONS

NOTES

PODCAST ((ᵠ)) WORKFLOW

GUEST

IDENTIFY & BOOK ◯

SEND PODCAST INFO ◯

SET RECORDING DATE ◯

DATE _____ TIME _____

RECORD EPISODE _____ ◯

EDIT EPISODE _____ ◯

SHOW NOTES/ ARTWORK _____ ◯

PUBLISH EPISODE _____ ◯

PROMOTE EPISODE _____ ◯

_____

_____

EPISODE TITLE		EPISODE #	DURATION	PUBLISH DATE

TOPIC/THEME	GUEST(s)	CONTACT INFO

🎙 SHOW INTRO

_____

_____

_____

_____

_____

_____

☆ GUEST/TOPIC INTRO

_____

_____

_____

_____

_____

_____

💬 QUESTIONS

_____

_____

_____

_____

_____

_____

_____

_____

_____

_____

_____

_____

_____

✎ NOTES

_____

_____

_____

_____

_____

_____

_____

_____

_____

_____

_____

_____

_____

_____

_____

_____

_____

_____

⚯ SPONSOR INFO

PODCAST ((ᵩ)) WORKFLOW

GUEST

   IDENTIFY & BOOK ⭕

   SEND PODCAST INFO ⭕

   SET RECORDING DATE ⭕

   DATE _____ TIME _____

RECORD EPISODE _____ ⭕

EDIT EPISODE _____ ⭕

SHOW NOTES/ ARTWORK _____ ⭕

PUBLISH EPISODE _____ ⭕

PROMOTE EPISODE _____ ⭕

_____

_____

EPISODE TITLE		EPISODE #	DURATION	PUBLISH DATE

TOPIC/THEME	GUEST(s)	CONTACT INFO

🎤 SHOW INTRO

_____

_____

_____

_____

_____

_____

⭐ GUEST/TOPIC INTRO

_____

_____

_____

_____

_____

_____

💬 QUESTIONS

_____

_____

_____

_____

_____

_____

_____

_____

_____

_____

_____

_____

✎ NOTES

_____

_____

_____

_____

_____

_____

_____

_____

_____

_____

_____

_____

_____

_____

_____

_____

_____

_____

_____

_____

⤳ SPONSOR INFO

PODCAST ((ᵠ)) WORKFLOW

GUEST

    IDENTIFY & BOOK   ◯

    SEND PODCAST INFO   ◯

    SET RECORDING DATE   ◯

    DATE _____ TIME _____

RECORD EPISODE _____ ◯

EDIT EPISODE _____ ◯

SHOW NOTES/ ARTWORK _____ ◯

PUBLISH EPISODE _____ ◯

PROMOTE EPISODE _____ ◯

_____

_____

EPISODE TITLE		EPISODE #	DURATION	PUBLISH DATE

TOPIC/THEME	GUEST(s)	CONTACT INFO

🎙️ SHOW INTRO

_____
_____
_____
_____
_____
_____

⭐ GUEST/TOPIC INTRO

_____
_____
_____
_____
_____
_____

💬 QUESTIONS

_____
_____
_____
_____
_____
_____
_____
_____
_____
_____
_____

_____   _____
_____   _____
_____   _____
_____   _____
_____   _____
_____   _____
_____   _____
_____   _____
_____   _____
_____   _____
_____   _____
_____   _____
_____   _____
_____   _____
_____   _____
_____   _____
_____   _____
_____   _____

⤳ SPONSOR INFO

PODCAST ((ᵩ)) WORKFLOW

GUEST

IDENTIFY & BOOK ○

SEND PODCAST INFO ○

SET RECORDING DATE ○

DATE _____ TIME _____

RECORD EPISODE _____ ○

EDIT EPISODE _____ ○

**SHOW NOTES/
ARTWORK** _____ ○

PUBLISH EPISODE _____ ○

PROMOTE EPISODE _____ ○

_____

_____

EPISODE TITLE		EPISODE #	DURATION	PUBLISH DATE

TOPIC/THEME	GUEST(s)	CONTACT INFO

🎙 SHOW INTRO

☆ GUEST/TOPIC INTRO

💬 QUESTIONS

NOTES

PODCAST ((ﾟ)) WORKFLOW

GUEST

IDENTIFY & BOOK ◯

SEND PODCAST INFO ◯

SET RECORDING DATE ◯

DATE _____ TIME _____

RECORD EPISODE _____ ◯

EDIT EPISODE _____ ◯

**SHOW NOTES/
ARTWORK** _____ ◯

PUBLISH EPISODE _____ ◯

PROMOTE EPISODE _____ ◯

EPISODE TITLE		EPISODE #	DURATION	PUBLISH DATE

TOPIC/THEME	GUEST(s)	CONTACT INFO

🎙 SHOW INTRO

_____
_____
_____
_____
_____
_____

☆ GUEST/TOPIC INTRO

_____
_____
_____
_____
_____
_____

💬 QUESTIONS

_____
_____
_____
_____
_____
_____
_____
_____
_____
_____
_____
_____

✎ NOTES

_____
_____
_____
_____
_____
_____
_____
_____
_____
_____
_____
_____
_____
_____
_____
_____
_____
_____
_____
_____
_____
_____

⤙ SPONSOR INFO

PODCAST ((ᵱ)) WORKFLOW

GUEST

IDENTIFY & BOOK ◯

SEND PODCAST INFO ◯

SET RECORDING DATE ◯

DATE _____ TIME _____

RECORD EPISODE _____ ◯

EDIT EPISODE _____ ◯

**SHOW NOTES/
ARTWORK** _____ ◯

PUBLISH EPISODE _____ ◯

PROMOTE EPISODE _____ ◯

_____
_____

EPISODE TITLE		EPISODE #	DURATION	PUBLISH DATE

TOPIC/THEME	GUEST(s)	CONTACT INFO

🎙 SHOW INTRO

_____
_____
_____
_____
_____
_____

⭐ GUEST/TOPIC INTRO

_____
_____
_____
_____
_____

💬 QUESTIONS

_____
_____
_____
_____
_____
_____
_____
_____
_____
_____
_____
_____

_____
_____
_____
_____
_____
_____
_____
_____
_____
_____
_____
_____
_____
_____
_____
_____
_____
_____
_____
_____
_____

⚇ SPONSOR INFO	PODCAST ((ᛎ)) WORKFLOW

GUEST

IDENTIFY & BOOK ◯

SEND PODCAST INFO ◯

SET RECORDING DATE ◯

DATE _____ TIME _____

RECORD EPISODE _____ ◯

EDIT EPISODE _____ ◯

SHOW NOTES/ ARTWORK _____ ◯

PUBLISH EPISODE _____ ◯

PROMOTE EPISODE _____ ◯

_____
_____

EPISODE TITLE		EPISODE #	DURATION	PUBLISH DATE

TOPIC/THEME	GUEST(s)	CONTACT INFO

🎤 SHOW INTRO

⭐ GUEST/TOPIC INTRO

💬 QUESTIONS

NOTES

PODCAST ((ɼ)) WORKFLOW

GUEST

IDENTIFY & BOOK ◯

SEND PODCAST INFO ◯

SET RECORDING DATE ◯

DATE _____ TIME _____

RECORD EPISODE _____ ◯

EDIT EPISODE _____ ◯

**SHOW NOTES/
ARTWORK** _____ ◯

PUBLISH EPISODE _____ ◯

PROMOTE EPISODE _____ ◯

_____

_____

EPISODE TITLE		EPISODE #	DURATION	PUBLISH DATE

TOPIC/THEME	GUEST(s)	CONTACT INFO

🎙 SHOW INTRO

_____

_____

_____

_____

_____

_____

⭐ GUEST/TOPIC INTRO

_____

_____

_____

_____

_____

_____

💬 QUESTIONS

_____

_____

_____

_____

_____

_____

_____

_____

_____

_____

_____

_____

✎ NOTES

_____
_____
_____
_____
_____
_____
_____
_____
_____
_____
_____
_____
_____
_____
_____
_____
_____
_____
_____
_____

✦ SPONSOR INFO

PODCAST ((ǫ)) WORKFLOW

GUEST

    IDENTIFY & BOOK ⬤

    SEND PODCAST INFO ⬤

    SET RECORDING DATE ⬤

    DATE _____ TIME _____

RECORD EPISODE _____ ⬤

EDIT EPISODE _____ ⬤

**SHOW NOTES/
ARTWORK** _____ ⬤

PUBLISH EPISODE _____ ⬤

PROMOTE EPISODE _____ ⬤

_____

_____

EPISODE TITLE		EPISODE #	DURATION	PUBLISH DATE

TOPIC/THEME	GUEST(s)	CONTACT INFO

🎙 SHOW INTRO

☆ GUEST/TOPIC INTRO

💬 QUESTIONS

✎ NOTES

_____
_____
_____
_____
_____
_____
_____
_____
_____
_____
_____
_____
_____
_____
_____
_____
_____
_____
_____
_____
_____

⋖ SPONSOR INFO

PODCAST ((•)) WORKFLOW

GUEST

    IDENTIFY & BOOK ⭘

    SEND PODCAST INFO ⭘

    SET RECORDING DATE ⭘

    DATE _____ TIME _____

RECORD EPISODE _____ ⭘

EDIT EPISODE _____ ⭘

**SHOW NOTES/
ARTWORK** _____ ⭘

PUBLISH EPISODE _____ ⭘

PROMOTE EPISODE _____ ⭘

_____
_____

EPISODE TITLE		EPISODE #	DURATION	PUBLISH DATE

TOPIC/THEME	GUEST(s)	CONTACT INFO

🎙 SHOW INTRO

⭐ GUEST/TOPIC INTRO

💬 QUESTIONS

✎ NOTES

___

⌁ SPONSOR INFO

PODCAST ((ϙ)) WORKFLOW

GUEST

    IDENTIFY & BOOK ◯

    SEND PODCAST INFO ◯

    SET RECORDING DATE ◯

    DATE _____ TIME _____

RECORD EPISODE _____ ◯

EDIT EPISODE _____ ◯

**SHOW NOTES/
ARTWORK** _____ ◯

PUBLISH EPISODE _____ ◯

PROMOTE EPISODE _____ ◯

___
___

EPISODE TITLE		EPISODE #	DURATION	PUBLISH DATE

TOPIC/THEME	GUEST(s)	CONTACT INFO

🎙 **SHOW INTRO**

_____
_____
_____
_____
_____
_____

☆ **GUEST/TOPIC INTRO**

_____
_____
_____
_____
_____
_____

💬 **QUESTIONS**

_____
_____
_____
_____
_____
_____
_____
_____
_____
_____
_____
_____

NOTES

SPONSOR INFO

PODCAST ((ᵠ)) WORKFLOW

GUEST

IDENTIFY & BOOK ⬭

SEND PODCAST INFO ⬭

SET RECORDING DATE ⬭

DATE _____ TIME _____

RECORD EPISODE _____ ⬭

EDIT EPISODE _____ ⬭

**SHOW NOTES/
ARTWORK** _____ ⬭

PUBLISH EPISODE _____ ⬭

PROMOTE EPISODE _____ ⬭

EPISODE TITLE		EPISODE #	DURATION	PUBLISH DATE

TOPIC/THEME	GUEST(s)	CONTACT INFO

🎙 SHOW INTRO

_____
_____
_____
_____
_____
_____

☆ GUEST/TOPIC INTRO

_____
_____
_____
_____
_____

💬 QUESTIONS

_____
_____
_____
_____
_____
_____
_____
_____
_____
_____
_____

PODCAST ((•)) WORKFLOW

GUEST

IDENTIFY & BOOK ◯

SEND PODCAST INFO ◯

SET RECORDING DATE ◯

DATE _____ TIME _____

RECORD EPISODE _____ ◯

EDIT EPISODE _____ ◯

SHOW NOTES/ ARTWORK _____ ◯

PUBLISH EPISODE _____ ◯

PROMOTE EPISODE _____ ◯

_____

_____

EPISODE TITLE		EPISODE #	DURATION	PUBLISH DATE

TOPIC/THEME	GUEST(s)	CONTACT INFO

🎙 SHOW INTRO

_____
_____
_____
_____
_____
_____

☆ GUEST/TOPIC INTRO

_____
_____
_____
_____
_____

💬 QUESTIONS

_____
_____
_____
_____
_____
_____
_____
_____
_____
_____
_____

✎ NOTES

_____

_____

_____

_____

_____

_____

_____

_____

_____

_____

_____

_____

_____

_____

_____

_____

_____

_____

_____

⌁ SPONSOR INFO

PODCAST ((ɸ)) WORKFLOW

GUEST

IDENTIFY & BOOK ◯

SEND PODCAST INFO ◯

SET RECORDING DATE ◯

DATE _____ TIME _____

RECORD EPISODE _____ ◯

EDIT EPISODE _____ ◯

SHOW NOTES/ ARTWORK _____ ◯

PUBLISH EPISODE _____ ◯

PROMOTE EPISODE _____ ◯

_____

_____

EPISODE TITLE		EPISODE #	DURATION	PUBLISH DATE

TOPIC/THEME	GUEST(s)	CONTACT INFO

🎤 **SHOW INTRO**

_____

_____

_____

_____

_____

_____

⭐ **GUEST/TOPIC INTRO**

_____

_____

_____

_____

_____

💬 **QUESTIONS**

_____

_____

_____

_____

_____

_____

_____

_____

_____

_____

_____

_____

_____

✎ NOTES

PODCAST ((ᵠ)) WORKFLOW

GUEST

    IDENTIFY & BOOK ⭕

    SEND PODCAST INFO ⭕

    SET RECORDING DATE ⭕

    DATE _____ TIME _____

RECORD EPISODE _____ ⭕

EDIT EPISODE _____ ⭕

SHOW NOTES/ ARTWORK _____ ⭕

PUBLISH EPISODE _____ ⭕

PROMOTE EPISODE _____ ⭕

EPISODE TITLE		EPISODE #	DURATION	PUBLISH DATE

TOPIC/THEME	GUEST(s)	CONTACT INFO

🎙 SHOW INTRO

⭐ GUEST/TOPIC INTRO

💬 QUESTIONS

NOTES

SPONSOR INFO

PODCAST ((ᵠ)) WORKFLOW

GUEST

    IDENTIFY & BOOK   ◯

    SEND PODCAST INFO   ◯

    SET RECORDING DATE   ◯

    DATE _____ TIME _____

RECORD EPISODE _____ ◯

EDIT EPISODE _____ ◯

SHOW NOTES/ ARTWORK _____ ◯

PUBLISH EPISODE _____ ◯

PROMOTE EPISODE _____ ◯

_____

_____

EPISODE TITLE		EPISODE #	DURATION	PUBLISH DATE

TOPIC/THEME	GUEST(s)	CONTACT INFO

🎤 SHOW INTRO

_____
_____
_____
_____
_____
_____

☆ GUEST/TOPIC INTRO

_____
_____
_____
_____
_____
_____

💬 QUESTIONS

_____
_____
_____
_____
_____
_____
_____
_____
_____
_____
_____
_____
_____

✎ NOTES

_____

_____

_____

_____

_____

_____

_____

_____

_____

_____

_____

_____

_____

_____

_____

_____

_____

_____

_____

_____

⤳ SPONSOR INFO

PODCAST ((ρ)) WORKFLOW

GUEST

    IDENTIFY & BOOK ◯

    SEND PODCAST INFO ◯

    SET RECORDING DATE ◯

    DATE _____ TIME _____

RECORD EPISODE _____ ◯

EDIT EPISODE _____ ◯

SHOW NOTES/ ARTWORK _____ ◯

PUBLISH EPISODE _____ ◯

PROMOTE EPISODE _____ ◯

_____

_____

EPISODE TITLE		EPISODE #	DURATION	PUBLISH DATE

TOPIC/THEME	GUEST(s)	CONTACT INFO

🎙 SHOW INTRO

⭐ GUEST/TOPIC INTRO

💬 QUESTIONS

NOTES

SPONSOR INFO

PODCAST ((ϙ)) WORKFLOW

GUEST

IDENTIFY & BOOK ◯

SEND PODCAST INFO ◯

SET RECORDING DATE ◯

DATE _____ TIME _____

RECORD EPISODE _____ ◯

EDIT EPISODE _____ ◯

**SHOW NOTES/
ARTWORK** _____ ◯

PUBLISH EPISODE _____ ◯

PROMOTE EPISODE _____ ◯

_____

_____

EPISODE TITLE		EPISODE #	DURATION	PUBLISH DATE

TOPIC/THEME	GUEST(s)	CONTACT INFO

🎙 SHOW INTRO

_____
_____
_____
_____
_____
_____

☆ GUEST/TOPIC INTRO

_____
_____
_____
_____
_____
_____

💬 QUESTIONS

_____
_____
_____
_____
_____
_____
_____
_____
_____
_____
_____
_____

_____
_____
_____
_____
_____
_____
_____
_____
_____
_____
_____
_____
_____
_____
_____
_____
_____
_____
_____
_____
_____

SPONSOR INFO

PODCAST ((ᵩ)) WORKFLOW

GUEST

IDENTIFY & BOOK ◯

SEND PODCAST INFO ◯

SET RECORDING DATE ◯

DATE _____ TIME _____

RECORD EPISODE _____ ◯

EDIT EPISODE _____ ◯

**SHOW NOTES/
ARTWORK** _____ ◯

PUBLISH EPISODE _____ ◯

PROMOTE EPISODE _____ ◯

_____ _____

_____ _____

EPISODE TITLE		EPISODE #	DURATION	PUBLISH DATE

TOPIC/THEME	GUEST(s)	CONTACT INFO

🎙 SHOW INTRO

⭐ GUEST/TOPIC INTRO

💬 QUESTIONS

✎ NOTES

_____
_____
_____
_____
_____
_____
_____
_____
_____
_____
_____
_____
_____
_____
_____
_____
_____
_____
_____
_____
_____

⌁ SPONSOR INFO

PODCAST ((φ)) WORKFLOW

GUEST

IDENTIFY & BOOK ◯

SEND PODCAST INFO ◯

SET RECORDING DATE ◯

DATE _____ TIME _____

RECORD EPISODE _____ ◯

EDIT EPISODE _____ ◯

SHOW NOTES/ ARTWORK _____ ◯

PUBLISH EPISODE _____ ◯

PROMOTE EPISODE _____ ◯

_____

_____

EPISODE TITLE		EPISODE #	DURATION	PUBLISH DATE

TOPIC/THEME	GUEST(s)	CONTACT INFO

🎙️ SHOW INTRO

_____

_____

_____

_____

_____

_____

☆ GUEST/TOPIC INTRO

_____

_____

_____

_____

_____

_____

💬 QUESTIONS

_____

_____

_____

_____

_____

_____

_____

_____

_____

_____

_____

_____

_____

✎ NOTES

PODCAST ((ꞯ)) WORKFLOW

GUEST

IDENTIFY & BOOK ◯

SEND PODCAST INFO ◯

SET RECORDING DATE ◯

DATE _____ TIME _____

RECORD EPISODE _____ ◯

EDIT EPISODE _____ ◯

**SHOW NOTES/
ARTWORK** _____ ◯

PUBLISH EPISODE _____ ◯

PROMOTE EPISODE _____ ◯

EPISODE TITLE		EPISODE #	DURATION	PUBLISH DATE

TOPIC/THEME	GUEST(s)	CONTACT INFO

🎙 SHOW INTRO

_____
_____
_____
_____
_____
_____

☆ GUEST/TOPIC INTRO

_____
_____
_____
_____
_____
_____

💬 QUESTIONS

_____
_____
_____
_____
_____
_____
_____
_____
_____
_____
_____
_____

NOTES

_____

_____

_____

_____

_____

_____

_____

_____

_____

_____

_____

_____

_____

_____

_____

_____

_____

_____

_____

_____

_____

SPONSOR INFO

PODCAST WORKFLOW

GUEST

    IDENTIFY & BOOK ◯

    SEND PODCAST INFO ◯

    SET RECORDING DATE ◯

    DATE _____ TIME _____

RECORD EPISODE _____ ◯

EDIT EPISODE _____ ◯

SHOW NOTES/ ARTWORK _____ ◯

PUBLISH EPISODE _____ ◯

PROMOTE EPISODE _____ ◯

_____

_____

EPISODE TITLE		EPISODE #	DURATION	PUBLISH DATE

TOPIC/THEME	GUEST(s)	CONTACT INFO

🎙 SHOW INTRO

_____

_____

_____

_____

_____

_____

☆ GUEST/TOPIC INTRO

_____

_____

_____

_____

_____

_____

💬 QUESTIONS

_____

_____

_____

_____

_____

_____

_____

_____

_____

_____

_____

_____

✎ NOTES

_____

_____

_____

_____

_____

_____

_____

_____

_____

_____

_____

_____

_____

_____

_____

_____

_____

_____

_____

⌁ SPONSOR INFO

PODCAST ((ᴘ)) WORKFLOW

GUEST

    IDENTIFY & BOOK ◯

    SEND PODCAST INFO ◯

    SET RECORDING DATE ◯

    DATE _____ TIME _____

RECORD EPISODE _____ ◯

EDIT EPISODE _____ ◯

SHOW NOTES/ ARTWORK _____ ◯

PUBLISH EPISODE _____ ◯

PROMOTE EPISODE _____ ◯

_____

_____

EPISODE TITLE		EPISODE #	DURATION	PUBLISH DATE

TOPIC/THEME	GUEST(s)	CONTACT INFO

🎙 SHOW INTRO

⭐ GUEST/TOPIC INTRO

💬 QUESTIONS

✎ NOTES

_____
_____
_____
_____
_____
_____
_____
_____
_____
_____
_____
_____
_____
_____
_____
_____
_____
_____
_____
_____
_____
_____

⚛ SPONSOR INFO

PODCAST ((ᵖ)) WORKFLOW

GUEST

IDENTIFY & BOOK ◯

SEND PODCAST INFO ◯

SET RECORDING DATE ◯

DATE _____ TIME _____

RECORD EPISODE _____ ◯

EDIT EPISODE _____ ◯

**SHOW NOTES/
ARTWORK** _____ ◯

PUBLISH EPISODE _____ ◯

PROMOTE EPISODE _____ ◯

_____
_____

EPISODE TITLE		EPISODE #	DURATION	PUBLISH DATE

TOPIC/THEME	GUEST(s)	CONTACT INFO

🎤 SHOW INTRO

_____
_____
_____
_____
_____
_____

⭐ GUEST/TOPIC INTRO

_____
_____
_____
_____
_____
_____

💬 QUESTIONS

_____
_____
_____
_____
_____
_____
_____
_____
_____
_____
_____
_____
_____

✎ **NOTES**

⤳ **SPONSOR INFO**

PODCAST ((ᴘ)) WORKFLOW

GUEST

IDENTIFY & BOOK ◯

SEND PODCAST INFO ◯

SET RECORDING DATE ◯

DATE _____ TIME _____

RECORD EPISODE _____ ◯

EDIT EPISODE _____ ◯

**SHOW NOTES/
ARTWORK** _____ ◯

PUBLISH EPISODE _____ ◯

PROMOTE EPISODE _____ ◯

_____ _____

_____ _____

EPISODE TITLE		EPISODE #	DURATION	PUBLISH DATE

TOPIC/THEME	GUEST(s)	CONTACT INFO

🎤 SHOW INTRO

⭐ GUEST/TOPIC INTRO

💬 QUESTIONS

✎ NOTES

⌁ SPONSOR INFO

PODCAST ((ꞁ)) WORKFLOW

GUEST

IDENTIFY & BOOK ◯

SEND PODCAST INFO ◯

SET RECORDING DATE ◯

DATE _____ TIME _____

RECORD EPISODE _____ ◯

EDIT EPISODE _____ ◯

**SHOW NOTES/
ARTWORK** _____ ◯

PUBLISH EPISODE _____ ◯

PROMOTE EPISODE _____ ◯

_____

_____

EPISODE TITLE		EPISODE #	DURATION	PUBLISH DATE

TOPIC/THEME	GUEST(s)	CONTACT INFO

🎙 SHOW INTRO

_____
_____
_____
_____
_____
_____

☆ GUEST/TOPIC INTRO

_____
_____
_____
_____
_____
_____

💬 QUESTIONS

_____
_____
_____
_____
_____
_____
_____
_____
_____
_____
_____
_____

_____
_____
_____
_____
_____
_____
_____
_____
_____
_____
_____
_____
_____
_____
_____
_____
_____
_____
_____
_____
_____

⚗ SPONSOR INFO

PODCAST ((ᵩ)) WORKFLOW

GUEST

IDENTIFY & BOOK ◯

SEND PODCAST INFO ◯

SET RECORDING DATE ◯

DATE _____ TIME _____

RECORD EPISODE _____ ◯

EDIT EPISODE _____ ◯

SHOW NOTES/ ARTWORK _____ ◯

PUBLISH EPISODE _____ ◯

PROMOTE EPISODE _____ ◯

_____
_____

EPISODE TITLE		EPISODE #	DURATION	PUBLISH DATE

TOPIC/THEME	GUEST(s)	CONTACT INFO

🎙 SHOW INTRO

☆ GUEST/TOPIC INTRO

💬 QUESTIONS

✎ NOTES

✂ SPONSOR INFO

PODCAST ((📡)) WORKFLOW

GUEST

    IDENTIFY & BOOK ⭕

    SEND PODCAST INFO ⭕

    SET RECORDING DATE ⭕

    DATE _____ TIME _____

RECORD EPISODE _____ ⭕

EDIT EPISODE _____ ⭕

SHOW NOTES/ ARTWORK _____ ⭕

PUBLISH EPISODE _____ ⭕

PROMOTE EPISODE _____ ⭕

EPISODE TITLE		EPISODE #	DURATION	PUBLISH DATE

TOPIC/THEME	GUEST(s)	CONTACT INFO

🎙 SHOW INTRO

_____
_____
_____
_____
_____
_____

☆ GUEST/TOPIC INTRO

_____
_____
_____
_____
_____

💬 QUESTIONS

_____
_____
_____
_____
_____
_____
_____
_____
_____
_____
_____

NOTES

_____

_____

_____

_____

_____

_____

_____

_____

_____

_____

_____

_____

_____

_____

_____

_____

_____

_____

_____

SPONSOR INFO

PODCAST ((ᵩ)) WORKFLOW

GUEST

IDENTIFY & BOOK ◯

SEND PODCAST INFO ◯

SET RECORDING DATE ◯

DATE _____ TIME _____

RECORD EPISODE _____ ◯

EDIT EPISODE _____ ◯

**SHOW NOTES/
ARTWORK** _____ ◯

PUBLISH EPISODE _____ ◯

PROMOTE EPISODE _____ ◯

_____

_____

EPISODE TITLE		EPISODE #	DURATION	PUBLISH DATE

TOPIC/THEME	GUEST(s)	CONTACT INFO

🎤 SHOW INTRO

_____
_____
_____
_____
_____
_____

⭐ GUEST/TOPIC INTRO

_____
_____
_____
_____
_____
_____

💬 QUESTIONS

_____
_____
_____
_____
_____
_____
_____
_____
_____
_____
_____
_____

PODCAST ((ᵩ)) WORKFLOW

GUEST

IDENTIFY & BOOK ○

SEND PODCAST INFO ○

SET RECORDING DATE ○

DATE _____ TIME _____

RECORD EPISODE _____ ○

EDIT EPISODE _____ ○

SHOW NOTES/ ARTWORK _____ ○

PUBLISH EPISODE _____ ○

PROMOTE EPISODE _____ ○

_____

_____

 Podcasting Basics

Podcasting is a great way to build an audience online. Not only do listeners become familiar with your expertise, but they're also introduced to your personal style and delivery. Podcasting also falls nicely into the exercise of acquiring expertise and giving it away as a strategy for becoming a recognized expert in your field.

All in all, podcasting is a great way to position yourself as an authority and find an audience of people interested in exactly what you have to offer.

It's one platform where the technical barriers to entry are pretty low. Here are the tools necessary to begin podcasting:

* USB Microphone with Foam Pop Filter
* Free/Low Cost Audio Recording Software
* RSS/Podcast Hosting Account

Thankfully, none of this stuff is really expensive and you can easliy get the basics setup within an hour or two.

Let's discuss the steps involved in recording your first podcast. Keep in mind, I went through this entire process in about 12 hours when I first got started. I discovered podcasting on the same day I recorded and posted my very first one. I say that to assure you it's just not that hard if you just put your head down and get it done. But, with the following tips, you'll save some time down the road.

Outline Episodes

The first thing you should do is write an outline for the first 10 episodes. That might seem pretty daunting at first, but don't be intimidated. I'm talking about a title and three or four bullet points for each episode. Nothing fancy. You got this!

The purpose is to get an idea how your expertise will unfold in the series. Each episode should build on previous episodes, allowing your audience to learn in a chronological way. It also encourages them to subscribe to your series, automatically receiving future episodes as they become available. In the beginning, I would plan on posting one episode each week if possible. It's crucial to satisfy your new audience's demand for fresh content. You may hook them with your first episode, but not be able to hold them if you wait too long to publish another.

Script the First Episode

You should already have an outline and this step requires you to beef it up enough to begin recording. Sometimes I write out the entire episode as a Word or Google document. I type pretty quickly and the process allows me to organize my thoughts. Once I'm finished, I go back and add paragraphs where additional explanation is necessary. This may not be required for everyone. You might be able to speak freestyle with only a few notes in front of you. This is ideal, as you will sound more natural.

Pick a Format

We'll dive into format options in the next chaper, but it's key to determine what kind of a podcast you plan to produce.

- Solo Host - Monologue
- Multiple Hosts - Dialogue
- Interview Format
- Documentary Style (think NPR podcasts which feature incredible sound design with music cues and sound effects to bring life to great stories)

Record & Publish

Once you've made and edited your recording, upload the MP3 file to your RSS hosting account and then register the feed URL with iTunes and other podcasting platforms. You'll need an account to submit your feed but it'll only take you a minute or two. I would also register the feed with some of the top podcast directories. Don't forget to promote your show on your social media platforms.

Podcasting is nice because listeners can find you on their own. Now, if your content is weak, they'll abandon your series as quickly as they joined. But if you have quality content, you'll be surprised how quickly you can develop an audience. Give it a try and get ready for a fascinating journey!

 Choosing the Right Format

You may have a great topic for your podcast and solid content, but for a podcast to be its best, you should come up with a specific format for your show and, for the most part, stick to it.

There are many things that make up the format of a podcast. The two I'll cover are the parts, or segments that make up a podcast, and the style you decide upon.

Podcast Segments

If you listen to a radio show, you'll often hear news at the top of the hour, then sports, then weather, back into music for a several minutes, then a commercial break, a listener's phone call, back into music, etc.

Together, all of those parts make up the show. While podcasting gives you the freedom to do whatever you want, whenever you want, most people are more comfortable when they have an idea of what's going on — in this case, I'm talking about your listeners.

Familiarity allows your listeners to not think about the format and just enjoy the content. And while you don't have to lock yourself into something precise, it's a good idea to map out how your show will generally flow.

Here's how one of my latest podcasts is formatted:

Teaser: Short soundbite from upcoming show (could be from an interview) to provoke curiosity. Funny, revealing and/or shocking are hallmarks of a good teaser.

Intro: This is prerecorded with some music and tells what the show is called, what it's about and then introduces the host (me!).

Welcome and Teaser: A little bit of chit-chat from the host, and then a teaser about what topics will be covered in this episode of the podcast. If I have a guest/interview, this is where I'd promote what we'll be discussing.

Current News (optional): A look at the leading news and rumors from the past week including some editorial comments if needed.

Sponsor: If there's a paid sponsor of the show, it's mentioned here, otherwise the sponsor position is used to promote a product as an affiliate.

Main Content: This is the "meat and potatoes" of the podcast and will vary depending on your podcast topic. If you have a guest/interview, give them a great introduction. This intro must hook and hold your audience.

Online Resources: Talk about a resource online that's related to the main content and that the listeners will find useful or interesting. If you have a guest/interview, tell listeners where/how to connect with them.

Feedback: Answer questions from listeners and solicit feedback using email, recorded comment line, etc.

Outro: Usually pre recorded with some music, this is the final goodbye for this episode. Make sure to remind listeners to subscribe and comment on your podcast.

Everyday, pro-podcasters use similar segments to create popular content. One big advantage for me, the podcast creator, is I don't have to come up with something new each time — I already have the format. All I have to do is fill in the blanks with the new content.

Some people don't like the idea of a static format for a podcast — they feel it conflicts with the idea of a podcast being "by the people, for the people." But a podcast can still be personal while being formatted — and if you take a look at the top podcasts, almost all of them use a fairly steady format.

Podcast Style

The other type of podcast format you need to decide on is the style you'll use. For example, you could be very casual or strictly business-like. Or somewhere in between.

Unless you know your audience extremely well, I'd suggest against sounding like you're all business. That's not to say you can't use a podcast for business — you can! It just means that a podcast, like any other method of communication with your prospects or customers, can be used to build relationships. Being more personable will go a long way towards building that relationship.

Personality is Key!

In a never ending sea of podcasts, an honest, engaging personality is one of the determining factors of standing out. Don't be shy to reveal the true YOU.

These days, authenticity is a hot commodity. Thankfully, it's totally free. Just lean into the idea of sharing your unique point-of-view. Chances are, there is a hungry audience looking for a show just like yours.

Fly Solo or Partner Up?

You'll also need to decide whether to fly solo or podcast with a partner. When you're podcasting by yourself, it's much easier to make decisions — you don't have to bounce ideas off anyone. You can also record your podcast when it's most convenient for you – no juggling schedules with someone else.

However, it's usually much easier to create many episodes of a podcast when there are at least two people. And many listeners think a team approach is less boring than a monologue.

If you choose to go with an interview format, solo-hosting is a good choice. Not only can it help distinguish yourself as an expert in your field, it's great for personal brand building.

The decisions on how to format your podcast are, of course, up to you. The good news is that there are no wrong answers. Ultimately, it's your podcast and you can make it the way you want — and if you want to try different formats to see which feel best, you can do that, too.

Just don't let the decisions hold you back — it's better to get started and do some tweaking as you go than to never launch your podcast because you're overwhelmed with decisions.

Tips for Great Interviews

People love to hear an interesting conversation. Dialogue keeps things fluid and interesting. When you podcast solo, you miss out on that engaging aspect. However, interviewing guests can add that exciting element to your podcast.

Interviewing isn't as simple as asking a question and getting an answer. Great interviews are an artform. Here are a few tips for interviewing success.

1. Prepare for the interview. Make sure to do background research on your subject. Background research includes the 5 Ws and H (Who, What, Where, When, Why, How), previous media coverage your subject has received and obtaining bio sheets, if applicable.

If they've given previous interviews, make sure to familiarize yourself with them. As a bonus for your listeners and your guest, try to find new ways to ask the same questions. Don't be scared to venture off to new territories not covered in previous interviews.

The real interview gold comes from tapping into fresh subjects. If you can get your guest to share new and revealing information, your show will feature something exclusive...which is great for promotion!

2. Prepare your questions. Write down your questions in advance and make sure to organize them in a way that flows. BUT, be flexible during the interview. Don't feel like you need to stick to the list. Let the conversation be your guide.

3. Prepare to actively listen. When newbie interviewers have questions written down, they tend not to listen to the guest's answers. They just ask another question and move on. When you truly listen to the answers, you'll come up with more questions that will add depth and excitement to your interview. Sometimes, the real magic is in the unscripted follow-up question. But, it's essential to actively listen to hear those opportunities.

4. Prepare your guest. You'll get a much better interview if your guest is prepared as well. Before you start, be sure to inform your guest of the types of things that will be discussed. Don't give them each question word-for-word, because that will give your interview a scripted tone.

The best answers usually come after the first time the question is asked. It's hard to near-impossible to recapture the energy and emotion of the first response to a question. Don't waste it if you're not recording.

Remember, what's recorded is what's remembered by your audience. However, give your guests a basic overview of the interview so they can prepare.

More Tips

One thing to remember is to always maintain control of the interview. Don't allow your guest to ramble. If they do, find a natural point to respecfully get them back on track.

Make sure to ask open ended questions. Avoid questions that begin with do you, have you, would you, could you. Closed-ended questions usually deliver a "yes" or "no" reply. How engaging is that for your listeners?

Avoid asking leading questions. Take your opinion out of the question before you ask. For example, if you ask, "Were you excited about the tour?" You'll either get a "Yes, I was excited" or "No, I wasn't excited". The guest will be focused on the word "excited". But if you ask, "How did you feel during the tour?", you'll get a much better answer.

If you don't get the answer you were hoping for, feel free to ask the question in a different way later in the interview.

Success leaves clues. Critically listen to an interview show you respect and take notes on how the host conducts their interview. Great interviews aren't accidental.

*Use the upcoming Podcast Planner forms to organize and prepare the necessary info for your show. After all, that's probably why you bought this book!

Producing Successful Shows

In learning anything new, there's always a learning curve and you're sure to make a few mistakes along the way. We all do! Don't let this derail your passion to podcast.

In order to save you some headaches along the way, here's a short list of common mistakes and how to avoid them in order to produce successful content.

Familiarizing yourself with them before pressing -Record- will allow you to enter the podcasting arena a few steps ahead of the competition.

<u>Reading From a Script</u>

While I strongly recommend writing an outline of what you want to cover in your podcast, it isn't necessary to read verbatim from a script. When most people try reading directly from a script, they wind up sounding like Ben Stein from the movie 'Ferris Bueller'. "Bueller? Bueller?" It isn't entertaining and you'll lose your audience before you even have a chance to get started. Unless you have a background in acting or extemporaneous performing, it's probably a good idea to forgo the script.

An easy solution is to make a list of talking points, note cards or even a more detailed outline of what you intend to say in your podcast. So long as the format leaves room for improvisation, it will come across as more friendly and conversational. It may take a few tries to get used to winging it, but you will sound much better.

It's still advisable to rehearse and edit your podcast whenever possible, but not to the point where it sounds too scripted or contrived. Natural with a few flubs always beats an overproduced show which can sound too polished and not authentic.

Sound Quality

While not everyone can afford really slick production values, it is important to appear at least somewhat professional. This means investing in a quality microphone, headphones and an audio editing program. Free audio editing apps include:

- Audacity (Windows & Mac)   • Garage Band (Mac)

This doesn't necessarily involve a large investment, though. The mic and headphones can be obtained for a reasonable amount, and you can download a free program like Audacity, which will allow you to edit your show. Audacity will allow you to lay down tracks of music, edit out coughs, ums, or even portions of the podcast you aren't happy with. It's alwasy best to cut out long pauses.

It's also worthwhile to do a sound check before spending 15 to 30 minutes recording a podcast that is unintelligible. Check that the mic volume is properly adjusted and that there isn't any background interference.

Infrequent Episodes

No one wants to subscribe to a show if it only airs sporadically. Why? Mainly because it's hard to maintain interest in a show if it isn't on enough to keep you engaged in the content. At the very least, try to release new shows every other week, if not weekly. It's true, some shows are only released monthly, but generally, the more frequently the show airs, the higher its rankings are.

No Call to Action

It's rare a listener will find your podcast only through your website. Most people will probably stumble across your podcast via a podcast directory. That's why it's important to make sure to include a call to action at the end of your show. If you don't provide a clear way for people to interact with you — they won't. Make sure to remind listeners to subscribe and leave a comment at the end of every show. You should also have this call-to-action in your podcast description.

No Show/Album Art

This only applies when submitting your podcasts to the various podcast directories and podcatchers. More often than not, people don't even take a second look at podcasts without good artwork. It doesn't have to be anything fancy and you can even use your logo as the album art, so long as it communicates something about the podcast.

Potential customers are looking for you through search engines, directories and forums. Give them a reason to choose your show versus all the other options. Common SEO (Search Engine Optimization) practices apply when completing your description.

Keep in mind, none of this has to be perfect. Don't let perfection stand in the way of progress. Every show you do, you'll become more adept at all aspects of the process. The biggest stumbling block for new podcasters is failure to stick to a consistent publishing schedule.

Instead of recording one show at a time, try to batch record a couple episodes on the same day. Audience building is challenging enough, position yourself for success by having enough new content for the first couple months.

Take time to brainstorm which niche you feel you have the most to offer and start coming up with show ideas. Create an avatar/picture of your typical listener. What are their pain points? What excites them? Create a podcast that authentically addresses their struggles and passions and you're more likely to quickly rack-up dedicated followers.

Bottomline: Don't overthink things. You wouldn't be reading this if you didn't have a spark of interest to start or up your podcasting game. Now more than ever, fresh voices are needed to deliver important messages.

You have a unique story to tell. Flip on your mic and boldly tell it!

To your podcasting success!

Use the Podcast Planning Forms to organize your show elements. Check out the QuickStart Guide on page 4 to familiarize yourself with the best way to use the forms. Nothing improves the quality of your podcast like taking the time to plan out each show before recording it. Not only will you be more relaxed, but you'll sound more like a podcasting pro!

Special Request

Your brief Amazon review could really help our family business. This link will take you to the Amazon.com review page for this book:

BadPermUnicorn.com/review57

Thank You!

Thanks so much for your purchase!

Made in the USA
Coppell, TX
23 April 2021

54367141R00069